Copyright © 2026 by GH WOOD LLC
All rights reserved. No part of this book may be reproduced in any manner whatsoever without written permission except in the case of brief quotations embodied in critical articles and reviews.
First Printing, 2026

US Politics Is for the Weak-Minded

US Politics Is for the Weak-Minded

Gary Haywood

AUTHOR'S DISCLAIMER

This book reflects the author's personal analysis, interpretations, and conclusions formed through independent study, lived observation, and direct experience. It is not written on behalf of any political party, ideology, organization, or movement. No affiliation, endorsement, or opposition is implied.

The perspectives presented here are diagnostic, not prescriptive. They are intended to examine structural patterns, incentives, and behaviors, not to promote activism, reform campaigns, or partisan solutions. This work does not seek consensus, emotional alignment, or validation. It seeks clarity.

Readers should understand that disagreement with the material is expected and appropriate. The arguments offered are not instructions to adopt specific beliefs, but frameworks to evaluate systems, behaviors, and personal assumptions. Responsibility for interpretation, agreement, or rejection remains entirely with the reader.

Nothing in this book should be construed as legal, financial, or political advice. The author does not claim authority beyond personal authorship and accountability for the ideas expressed.

This work is written from a standpoint that prioritizes individual responsibility, critical thinking, and operational agency. The intent is not to persuade readers to think *like* the author, but to think *for themselves*.

If the material challenges comfort, identity, or long-held assumptions, that discomfort is not a flaw of the work. It is a signal that examination is occurring.

INTRODUCTION

The Mistake We Keep Repeating

Corruption is not a modern discovery. It has existed as long as systems have existed. Every civilization that concentrated authority also concentrated incentives to abuse it. What *is* new is the level of tolerance we now extend toward it, and how seamlessly it has blended into daily life.

Modern politics no longer functions as a problem-solving mechanism. It functions as a perception-management system. Outcomes are secondary. Narratives are primary. The system rewards those who amplify emotion, signal alignment, and repeat approved language. Competence is optional. Restraint is inconvenient. Responsibility is actively discouraged. This is not a failure of design. It *is* the design.

Efficiency favors simplification. Simplification favors slogans. Slogans replace thinking.

As a result, political participation has been reduced to emotional compliance. Outrage substitutes for analysis. Identity substitutes for accountability. Voting substitutes for agency. People are encouraged to feel involved while remaining operationally passive. The appearance of engagement masks the absence of responsibility.

The most uncomfortable truth is not that institutions are corrupt.

It is that corruption survives because individuals tolerate it.

People demand reform while continuing the behaviors that make reform impossible. They condemn outcomes while rewarding the same inputs. They outsource responsibility upward, waiting for permission, leadership, or rescue, while quietly surrendering their own agency in the process. This dependency is not imposed. It is accepted.

The mistake we keep repeating is believing that systems change first and individuals follow. History shows the opposite. Systems reflect the behavior they aggregate. When individuals abandon discipline, systems decay. When individuals abdicate responsibility, authority concentrates. When individuals trade thinking for belonging, corruption becomes stable.

Nothing will change until individuals do.

This book does not promise solutions. It does not offer optimism. It does not attempt to motivate or inspire. Those approaches have already failed. Instead, this book provides diagnosis, clear, structural, and unsentimental.

Because before anything can be corrected, it must be understood.

And understanding is the first act of responsibility.

Chapter 1

Politics as a Substitute for Thinking

Nearly all political participation today is performative.

Voting, arguing, posting, and identifying feel productive but rarely are. These actions provide emotional release without requiring competence. The system encourages this because emotional engagement is easier to manage than independent thought.

Thinking independently requires:

Friction
Delay
Personal accountability
Acceptance of isolation
Politics offers the opposite:
Belonging
Certainty
Moral outsourcing
Identity without effort
This is not empowerment. It is sedation.

Chapter 2

Weak-Minded Is a Condition, Not an Insult

Weak-mindedness is not about intelligence.

It is about **dependency**. A weak-minded individual:

Defers judgment upward
Replaces responsibility with affiliation
Trades agency for reassurance
Confuses participation with progress

This condition is cultivated deliberately. Systems prefer predictable participants over capable individuals. Predictability is controllable. Independence is not.

Chapter 3

Corruption as a Systems Feature

Corruption persists because it works.

It concentrates power, simplifies decision-making, and reduces friction for those inside the system. Expecting a corrupt system to self-correct is irrational. Systems optimize for survival, not virtue.
The mistake is assuming corruption is a deviation.

It is not.

It is the natural outcome when individuals surrender responsibility and demand solutions without discipline.

Chapter 4

Emotional Alignment vs. Functional Reality

Emotion is cheap. Competence is not.

Political systems reward those who:

Signal alignment
Repeat approved narratives
Display outrage on command

They penalize those who:

Ask structural questions
Refuse emotional framing
Operate independently

This creates a population that feels informed while remaining ineffective.

Chapter 5

The Illusion of Reform

Reform is the most profitable lie in politics.

It keeps individuals invested while changing nothing fundamental. Each cycle promises correction while expanding complexity, bureaucracy, and distance from accountability.

Real reform would require:

Reduced dependence
Personal competence
Fewer intermediaries
Individual responsibility

These outcomes threaten the system.

Chapter 6

The Individual Is the Bottleneck

No political solution can compensate for widespread personal dysfunction.

Debt, dependency, poor discipline, emotional reasoning, and avoidance of responsibility cannot be legislated away. They must be corrected individually.

This is the core conflict:

Individuals want systemic fixes
Systems require individual discipline

Until this mismatch is resolved, corruption remains permanent.

Chapter 7

Operating Without Approval

Independent individuals do not wait for permission.

They:

Build skills
Reduce dependence
Avoid leverage
Operate quietly
Measure outcomes

This mirrors the same operating philosophy found in:

Self EMS (personal operating systems)

Mastering the Basics (discipline over motivation)

The Power of No Debt (avoiding structural traps)

The Learning Curve (functional adaptation)

Politics becomes irrelevant when individuals become competent.

Chapter 8

Why Nothing Changes

Nothing changes because change is uncomfortable.

It requires:

Sacrifice without applause
Delayed gratification
Rejection of identity politics
Acceptance of personal limits

Most people prefer the illusion of involvement to the burden of responsibility.

The Only Honest Answer

Corruption is abhorrent.

It is also predictable. It will not be solved through politics. It will not be fixed by leaders. It will not be corrected by outrage.

It ends only when individuals reclaim agency.

Nothing will change unless you change.
That is not pessimism.
That is reality.

EPILOGUE

Responsibility Has No Successor

This book ends where responsibility begins. There will be no final reform, no corrective election, no moment where the system suddenly recognizes its excesses and chooses restraint. Systems do not self-correct because of moral pressure. They correct only when the behaviors sustaining them change. Until then, corruption remains stable, not because it is powerful, but because it is tolerated.

The most persistent illusion in modern civic life is that responsibility can be delegated. That if the right person is elected, appointed, exposed, or removed, the problem will resolve itself. This belief is convenient. It preserves outrage while excusing participation. It allows individuals to condemn outcomes without interrogating their own role in sustaining the conditions that produce them.

Corruption is not sustained solely by those who benefit from it. It is sustained by those who accommodate it. By those who rationalize small compromises. By those who trade attention for outrage, comfort for silence, and agency for alignment. Over time, these choices accumulate. Not dramatically. Quietly. Systemically.

Nothing in this book requires agreement. It requires recognition. Recognition that modern politics functions less as a mechanism for problem-solving and more as a system for managing perception. Recognition that outrage has become a renewable resource, harvested and redirected, rarely resolved. Recognition that participation without accountability is not engagement, it is consumption.

This is not a call to activism. Activism without discipline becomes theater. This is not a call to optimism. Optimism without adjustment is denial. And this is not a call to despair. Despair still centers the system as all-powerful.

It is a call to sobriety.

To evaluate personal behavior with the same scrutiny applied to institutions. To recognize patterns, what is tolerated, repeated, excused, and ignored. To understand that every system, no matter how large, is composed of individual decisions operating in aggregate.

Responsibility does not scale upward. It scales inward. The system will continue to reward compliance, repetition, and emotional alignment. That is its function. But individuals are not obligated to mirror its incentives. Agency still exists, though it is rarely exercised because it demands cost without applause. No one is coming to fix this. And nothing is broken by accident.

What happens next depends less on reform and more on refusal, refusal to outsource responsibility, refusal to participate in cycles that require amnesia to function, refusal to confuse awareness with action.

This book offers no resolution because resolution is not collective. It is personal.

The question is no longer whether corruption exists.

The question is whether it is still being tolerated.

www.ingramcontent.com/pod-product-compliance
Lightning Source LLC
Chambersburg PA
CBHW060603030426
42337CB00019B/3589